VALERIAN

SCRIPT WILFRID LUPANO
ARTWORK AND COLOURS MATHIEU LAUFFRAY

CHARACTERS CREATED BY PIERRE CHRISTIN AND JEAN-CLAUDE MÉZIÈRES

CINEBOOK
The 9th Art Publisher

The first time we discussed the possibility of making this book was in 2013, during the exhibition of the last *Long John Silver*. It was a high point, believe me, because *Valerian* is a foundational series in my life as an author.

Which is why I want to offer my heartfelt thanks to Jean-Claude Mézières and his lifelong accomplice Pierre Christin, who gave me a fantastic gift that day. Thanks also to François Le Bescond and Philippe Ostermann, who believed in this project and gave it all their support.

My thanks to Anthony Simon for his invaluable help in preparing the colour pages. Further thanks to Gabriel Uribe, whose modelling of the Shingouz ship turned out to be extremely useful. A manly hug to my studio buddies Alex Alice and Patrick Pion; I think I was less of a pain on this book than I was on the previous ones – aside from my repeated chuckling… Finally, my thanks to Jean Bastide for sharing his knowledge of digital colouring.

Wilfrid and I did our best to prove ourselves up to the task, without ever trying to mimic the original series – as that would be pointless – but I want to express how exhilarating it was to bring to life, in our own way, that world and those heroes who made us dream all our lives. I truly hope that *Shingouzlooz Inc.* will give you a fine reading time!

M.L.

Original title: Valerian – Shingouzlooz Inc.
Original edition: © Dargaud Paris, 2017 by Lupano & Lauffray
www.dargaud.com
All rights reserved
English translation: © 2017 Cinebook Ltd
Translator: Jerome Saincantin
Editor: Erica Olson Jeffrey
Lettering and text layout: Design Amorandi
Printed in Spain by EGEDSA
This edition first published in Great Britain in 2018 by
Cinebook Ltd
56 Beech Avenue
Canterbury, Kent
CT4 7TA
www.cinebook.com
A CIP catalogue record for this book
is available from the British Library
ISBN 978-1-84918-401-4

9th CINEBOOK
The 9th Art Publisher

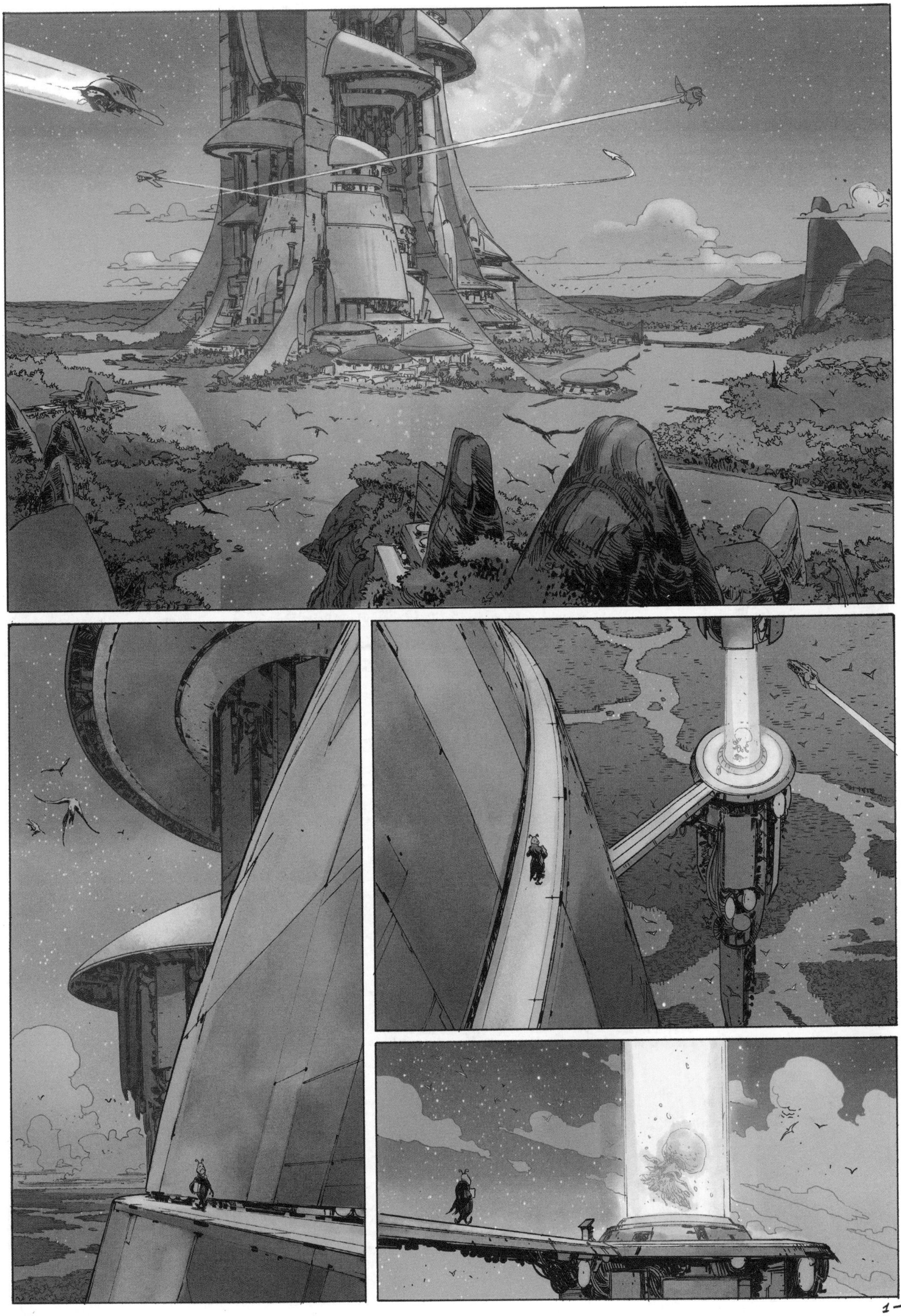

GOOD EVENING.
IT'S TIME. CASE
8222222789-2.

IT'S ABOUT TO START.

BLEEP
BLEEP...

ARE...
ARE WE
SURE?...

WE'LL KNOW
IN A MINUTE.

WHAT'S THE
TRIGGER?

A BLUE TUNA.

QUANTUM.

QUANTUM?

YES, QUANTUM.

YIKES. IT'S ALWAYS
TRICKY WHEN IT'S
QUANTUM...

MANY, MANY FACTORS.

YES, MANY...

LET ME HAVE A LOOK.

IT'S NEVER
GOOD WHEN IT'S
QUANTUM.

NO,
NEVER.

2-

SO, WHY DON'T WE HAVE A PICTURE OF THIS MYSTERIOUS MR ZI-PONE?

HE'S A CLASS 1 ANDROID.

HE SWITCHES HEADS OFTEN.

AND YET IT'S THAT HEAD WE WANT. HIS ARTIFICIAL BRAIN CONSISTS OF TWO SUPER-POWERFUL SERVERS, ST PERCENT AND GROSCERNIN.

THAT ROBOT CREATES OVER A MILLION ANONYMOUS COMPANIES EVERY DAY. HE NEVER STOPS WORKING.

BOTH HAVE BEEN RECOGNISED BY POINT CENTRAL AS SOVEREIGN STATES – MEANING IT'S POSSIBLE TO REGISTER A CORPORATION THERE.

SO, IF I UNDERSTAND CORRECTLY...

...WE'RE LOOKING FOR A TAX HAVEN IN THE MIDDLE OF A REGULAR HEAVEN.

EXACTLY.

BINGO! HE'S OVER THERE.

END OF THE LINE, MR ZI-PONE.

4–

THAT'S THE GALAXY'S FINANCIAL CRIMINAL MASTERMIND? HE LOOKS LIKE A WALKING SCRAP HEAP.

ARTIFICIAL INTELLIGENCES JUST LOVE THE WHOLE VINTAGE LOOK. DON'T LET IT FOOL YOU, THOUGH.

THAT OLD TIN CAN IS FILLED WITH MINIATURISED SENSORS AND TECHNOLOGY.

HE'S TOP OF THE LINE.

M'YEAH... IN THE MEANTIME, THERE HE IS FISHING WITH A STRING ON A STICK.

TAP! TAP! TAP!

THAT'S WHAT THEY CALL THE ANDROID PARADOX... THE MORE ADVANCED THEY ARE, THE MORE FASCINATED THEY ARE BY PRIMITIVE TECHNOLOGIES.

?..

FLAP! FLAP!

5.-

DON'T TRY ANYTHING, MR ZI-PONE. IN THE NAME OF THE LAW, I AM PLACING YOU UNDER ARREST FOR VIOLATING 378 INTERGALACTIC TAX AND BANKING LAWS.

OH?... THAT MANY?

FLAP. FLAP..

OH, YES. COME WITH US.

WAIT, CAN'T WE TALK ABOUT THIS? LOOK, THIS IS A NICE PLACE. D'YOU LIKE GRILLED FISH? I HAVE A MARINADE RECIPE...

YOU EAT GRILLED FISH? YOU?

NO, BUT YOU PROBABLY DO. SEE, THIS IS A QUANTUNA. A QUANTUM MIGRATION TUNA FROM VAHAMINE. THE MOST EXPENSIVE FISH IN THE UNIVERSE. IT'S WORTH SEVERAL YEARS OF YOUR SALARIES.

WHAT DO YOU KNOW OF OUR SALARIES?...

YOU MADE PHYSICAL CONTACT WITH ME. I ANALYSED YOUR DNA AND FOUND YOUR FILES IN GALAXITY'S SERVERS IN UNDER ONE SECOND.

WHAT?!

YOU... YOU HAVE ACCESS TO GALAXITY'S SERVERS? BUT THE SECURITY IS TOP-NOTCH!

YOU'RE KIDDING, RIGHT? SAY, YOUR SOCIAL SITUATION IS NOTHING TO WRITE HOME ABOUT. DO THEY REALLY PAY YOU SO LITTLE? WITH THE RISKS YOU TAKE?

WELL ...

AND I SUPPOSE YOU HAVEN'T PLANNED AHEAD, RETIREMENT-WISE?

RETIREMENT IS IMPORTANT, YOU KNOW. IF YOU'D LIKE, I CAN PUT A LITTLE SOMETHING TOGETHER FOR YOU WITH SOME START-UP CAPITAL.

RETIREM... ER...

8

THERE. WHILE WE WERE TALKING, I SOLD THIS QUANTUNA BY THE KILO ON THE INTERGALACTIC MARKET — FOR TWO THOUSAND TIMES YOUR ANNUAL SALARY.

WHAT!!? TWO THOUSAND...! THIS FISH HERE?!!

ABSOLUTELY. SO, HERE'S WHAT I PROPOSE: WITH YOUR FINE SHIP, YOU DELIVER THIS FRESH CATCH TO THE BUYER ON THE MOON OF USSAH-SHIM E WITHIN TWENTY-FOUR HOURS, AND I'LL DEPOSIT THE MONEY FOR YOU IN AN ACCOUNT ON MY SERVERS ST PERCENT AND GROSCERNIN...

...THROUGH A SECURITISATION PLAN AT 15% INDEXED TO THE PLANCKIAN RATE OF...

YOU DO REALISE THE QUANTUNA IS A PROTECTED SPECIES, OF COURSE...?

FLAP!

WELL, OF COURSE. WHY WOULD IT BE SO EXPENSIVE OTHERWISE?

TWO THOUSAND YEARS' SALARY...

HAVE YOU PUT A LITTLE SOME-THING ASIDE? DO YOU KNOW WHAT THE RETIREMENT PLAN IS FOR A SPATIO-TEMPORAL AGENT?

WELL...

ER... VALERIAN, CAN I TALK TO YOU FOR A SECOND?

THAT RUST BUCKET IS TRYING TO BRIBE YOU! CAN'T YOU SEE THAT THIS SCHEME OF HIS IS A SCAM?

YES, YES...

..BUT STILL, HE'S RIGHT THAT OUR PENSION—

CLICK!

ZZ!!!P!

!?....

GZZZTT

...!...

VALERIAN! LAURELINE!

HELP! HE'S GOING TO KILL US!

HELP US!

WH... WHAT?... THE SHINGOUZ?!! WHERE DID YOU COME FROM?

AND HOW DID YOU KNOW WHERE WE WERE?

WELL, SINCE YOU'RE SUCH GOOD CUSTOMERS, WE PUT A BEACON ON YOUR SHIP. EASIER THAT WAY.

ACHOOO!...

WHAT?! BUT GALAXITY'S SHIPS ARE PROTECTED AGAINST TRACKERS!!

YOU'RE KIDDING, RIGHT?...

YOU HAVE TO HELP US! HE'S BEEN HUNTING US ACROSS THE UNIVERSE!

SNIFF! GAD SEEB DO SHAKE HIB OFF! HE'S FURIOUS! HE'S LOSD HIS BIND!

WHO?!... WHO ARE YOU TALKING ABOUT?!

8-

WHAT NOW!?...

!!

ALREADY?!

?

THAT'S ...

YOU'RE NOT GETTING AWAY FROM ME, YOU GALACTIC COCKROACHES!!

...

?!

PEW! PEW! PEW!

BLOM! BLOM! BLOM!

YAAHHH

W... WAIT... HE'S...

TOTAL OBLITERATIONNNN!!!

ZI-PONE!!

HE... HE'S GONE MAD...

...M... MY...

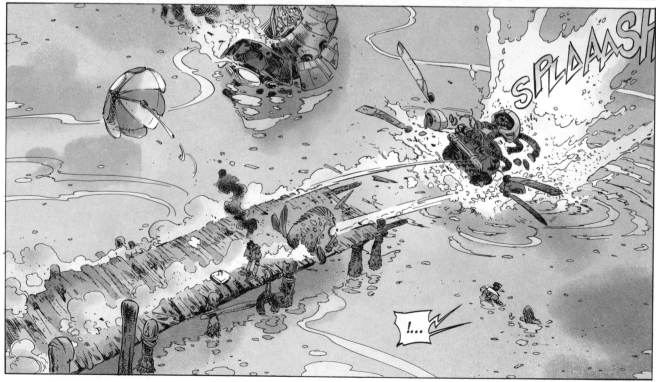

!....

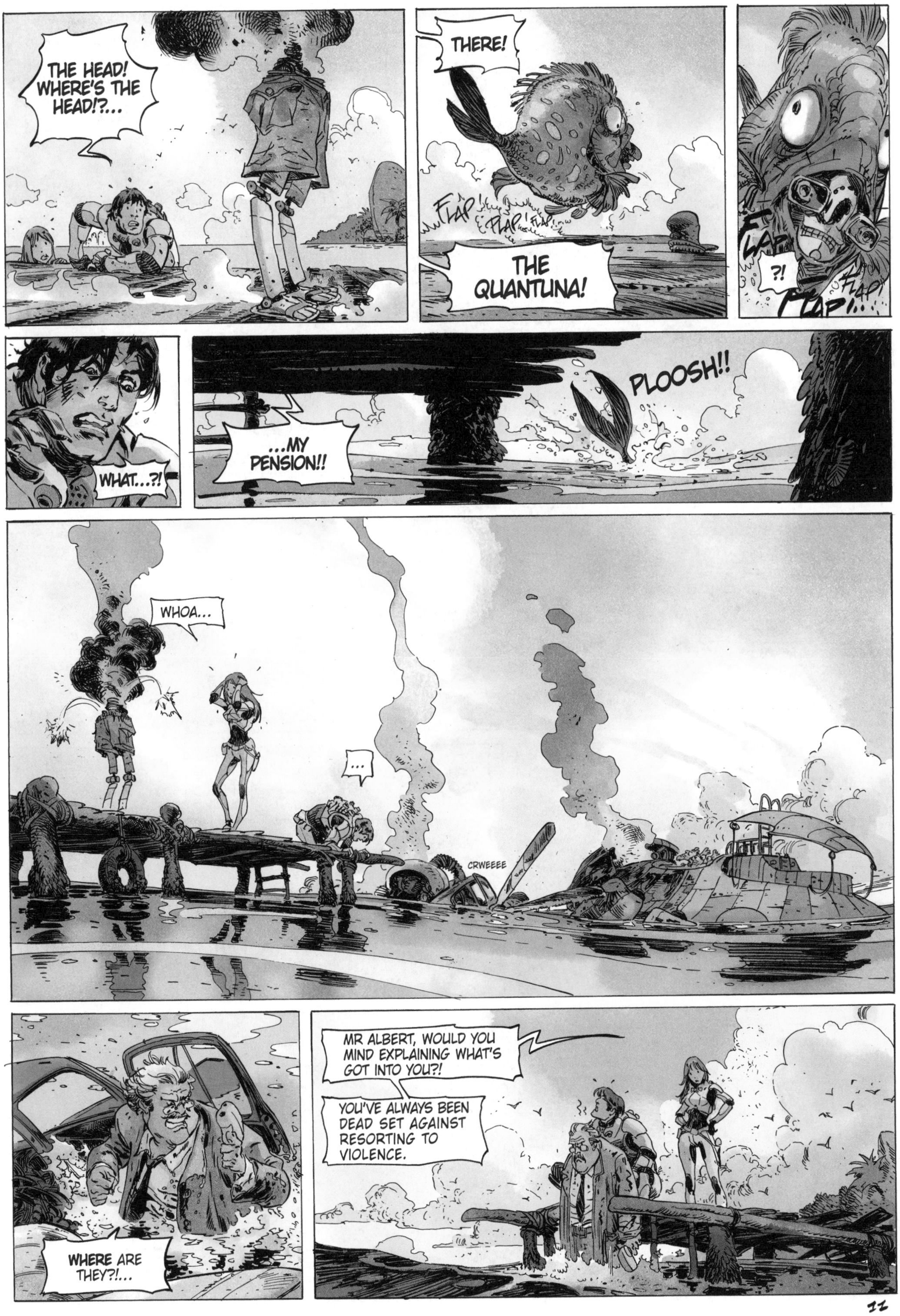
THE HEAD! WHERE'S THE HEAD!?...
THERE!
FLAP! FLAP! FLAP!
THE QUANTUNA!
FLAP
?!
FLAP! FLAP!
WHAT...?!
...MY PENSION!!
PLOOSH!!
WHOA...
...
CRWEEEE
WHERE ARE THEY?!...
MR ALBERT, WOULD YOU MIND EXPLAINING WHAT'S GOT INTO YOU?!
YOU'VE ALWAYS BEEN DEAD SET AGAINST RESORTING TO VIOLENCE.
11

OH, LOOK — YOU EQUIPPED YOUR OLD RENAULT 4 WITH A SPATIO-TEMPORAL TELEPORTER...?

LET ME AT THEM! I'M GOING TO ATOMISE THEM!!

MR ALBERT! THE SHINGOUZ ARE OUR FRIENDS, AND—

OUR FRIENDS?! THE WORST CREATURES IN THE UNIVERSE! EVIL INCARNATE! THAT'S WHAT THEY ARE!

MR ALBERT, PUT THE WEAPON DOWN. LOOK AT WHAT YOU'VE DONE ALREADY.

!

DEAR LORD!!

I'VE TAKEN A LIFE! IN FORTY YEARS OF SERVICE I'VE NEVER DONE SUCH A THING!

WHO? THAT PAIR OF SHORTS THERE? OH, NO, THAT WAS A ROBOT.

VALERIAN! HOW CAN YOU BE SO CASUAL?! DON'T YOU KNOW THAT ARTICLE 5, PARAGRAPH 3 OF THE GALACTIC CHARTER GRANTS ARTIFICIAL BEINGS THE STATUS OF INTELLIGENT AND SENTIENT LIFE-FORMS?

HMM... OH, YES, ER...

EVEN IF ARTIFICIAL, LIFE IS SACRED! I AM A MURDERER! I BETRAYED MY DUTY!

AND IT'S ALL THEIR FAULT!

YEAH, WELL, SHINGOUZ HAVE THAT WHOLE, NICE, WHATCHAMACALLIT STATUS THING TOO, YOU KNOW...

SENTIENT CREATURES, ALL THAT...

SO... SNIFF... EASY WITH THE BEW BEW...

WHAT IS IT THEY'VE DONE, ANYWAY?

I'LL LET THEM TELL YOU THEMSELVES.

WE'RE NOT ABOVE ADMITTING WE GOOFED UP...

12-

OK, SO, SOME TIME AGO WE CREATED 'SHINGOUZLOOZ INC.', A SMALL COMPANY SPECIALISED IN EXPLORING TAX-EXEMPT SPACE...

...TO DIVERSIFY A BIT.

THE COMPANY WAS GOING TO SEND BEACON-PROBES ALL OVER THE UNIVERSE TO LOOK FOR AS YET UNDISCOVERED AND UNCATALOGUED PLANETS.

ID'S THE OLD SYSDEM... SNIFF... WHED THEY FIND ONE, THE PROBES DIG IN AND SDARD EBIDDING A SIGNAL.

AD THAD BOIND, THE GOMBANY GAN SDAKE IDS GLAIM WITH DE BOIND CENDRAL INTER-GALAGTIG CHAMBER OB GOBBERCE...

...AD GAIDS OWDERSHIP OB DE PLANEDD.

I HATE STUFF LIKE THAT. IT'S STRAIGHT-UP COLONIALISM.

YES. A TERRAN INVENTION, AS IT HAPPENS...

THANKS FOR REMINDING ME.

I STILL DON'T SEE WHERE THE GOOF-UP IS.

JUST WAIT. IT'S A REAL HUMDINGER!

WELL, IT'S JUST THAT WE HAD THE IDEA OF USING A PATCHED-TOGETHER SPATIO-TEMPORAL TELEPORTER TO SEND OUR PROBES REALLY FAR OUT INTO SPACE...

DO SAVE DIBE, YOU KNOW...

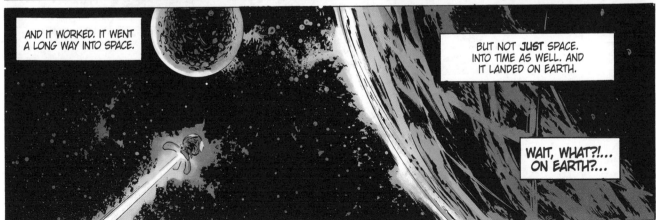

AND IT WORKED. IT WENT A LONG WAY INTO SPACE.

BUT NOT **JUST** SPACE. INTO TIME AS WELL. AND IT LANDED ON EARTH.

WAIT, WHAT?!... ON EARTH?...

73

...THAT'S A TERRAN INVENTION, TOO!

YES, BUT THE THING IS, THE PROBE WENT BACK A LONG, LONG TIME. BEFORE THE FORMATION OF LIFE ON EARTH — 3.5 BILLION YEARS.

WHAT?!

BEEP... BEEP...
BEEP... BEEP...
BEEP...

AND IT LANDED.

WAIT...

THAT DOESN'T MAKE SENSE. INTERGALACTIC LAWS PROHIBIT COLONISING ANY PLANET THAT ALREADY HARBOURS LIVING ORGANISMS. THE RIGHTS OF PEOPLE AND LIFE-FORMS TO SELF-DETERMINATION...

AND THEN IT STARTED EMITTING.

NO WAAAY...?!

AND THAT'S THE PROBLEM... 'CAUSE AT THE POINT CENTRAL INTERGALACTIC CHAMBER OF COMMERCE... TECHNICALLY SPEAK-ING... THE PROBE'S BEEN EMITTING FOR 3.5 BILLION YEARS...

...SO THEY VALIDATED OUR DEED OF PROPERTY. WHICH MEANS THAT EARTH ACTUALLY...

IT BELONGS TO YOU? IS THAT WHAT YOU'RE TRYING TO TELL US?!

OH, NO, NO, WAIT. THERE'S MORE...

YES, WELL... IT'S OURS... UH...

IN FACT, TECHNICALLY, IT BELONGS TO THAT COMPANY, SHINGOUZLOOZ INC.

WHICH IS YOURS, ISN'T IT?

YES, WELL, ID WAS OURS, DRUE... BUD...

THERE WAS THAT GARD GABE ONE NIGHD ON VEY-GUSS.

GARD GABE?

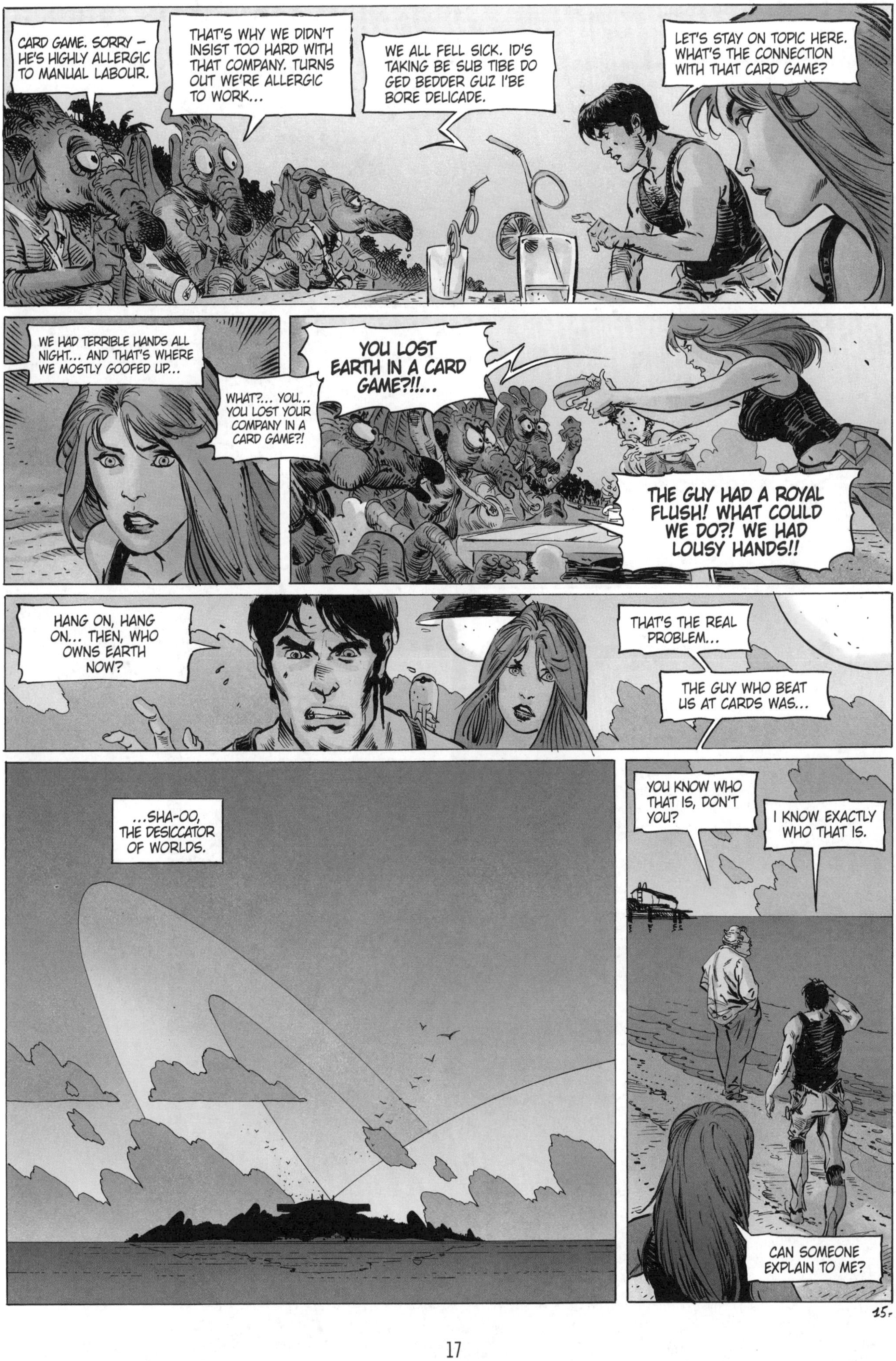

CARD GAME. SORRY – HE'S HIGHLY ALLERGIC TO MANUAL LABOUR.
THAT'S WHY WE DIDN'T INSIST TOO HARD WITH THAT COMPANY. TURNS OUT WE'RE ALLERGIC TO WORK...
WE ALL FELL SICK. ID'S TAKING BE SUB TIBE DO GED BEDDER GUZ I'BE BORE DELICADE.
LET'S STAY ON TOPIC HERE. WHAT'S THE CONNECTION WITH THAT CARD GAME?
WE HAD TERRIBLE HANDS ALL NIGHT... AND THAT'S WHERE WE MOSTLY GOOFED UP...
WHAT?... YOU... YOU LOST YOUR COMPANY IN A CARD GAME?!
YOU LOST EARTH IN A CARD GAME?!!...
THE GUY HAD A ROYAL FLUSH! WHAT COULD WE DO?! WE HAD LOUSY HANDS!!
HANG ON, HANG ON... THEN, WHO OWNS EARTH NOW?
THAT'S THE REAL PROBLEM...
THE GUY WHO BEAT US AT CARDS WAS...
...SHA-OO, THE DESICCATOR OF WORLDS.
YOU KNOW WHO THAT IS, DON'T YOU?
I KNOW EXACTLY WHO THAT IS.
CAN SOMEONE EXPLAIN TO ME?
15

SHA-OO THE DESICCATOR, THE POACHER OF SEAS.

HE CONTROLS A SCHOOL OF COLOSSAL CREATURES THAT LIVE IN THE VOID BETWEEN STARS AND FEED THEMSELVES BY SIPHONING OFF THE WATER FROM PLANETS THEY COME ACROSS.

TITANIC STELLAR VAMPIRES CAPABLE OF GULPING DOWN ENTIRE OCEANS.

THE DESICCATOR THEN RESELLS THAT WATER IN OTHER SYSTEMS WHERE WATER IS SCARCE, TO THE HIGHEST BIDDER – AND AT EXTORTIONATE PRICES.

IF SHA-OO HAS OBTAINED THE RIGHT TO TAP THE WATERS OF EARTH, WE'LL SOON BE ABLE TO CYCLE FROM BREST TO NEW YORK...

B... BUT SURELY SOMETHING CAN BE DONE! POINT CENTRAL'S NOT GOING TO SANCTION A GAMBLING DEBT, IS IT?!!

I CHECKED. THESE MORONS SIGNED A PROPER TRANSFER OF OWNERSHIP. IT'S ALL BY THE BOOK AND PERFECTLY LEGAL. POINT CENTRAL WASHES ITS COLLECTIVE HANDS OF IT.

THAT'S THE FINAL DRINKING STRAW RIGHT THERE, SHINGOUZ...

WE DIDN'T KNOW IT WAS EARTH WHEN WE SIGNED AWAY THE COMPANY!

ANYONE CAN MAKE A MISTAKE, RIGHT?

ACHOO!! REALLY SORRY...

16

I'VE GOT IT!

WE CAN USE THE SPACE-TIME COORDINATES TO WHICH THE PROBE WAS SENT TO TRAVEL BACK TO A LITTLE BEFORE IT ARRIVED AND DESTROY IT...

UM... I MUST POINT OUT THAT THE CODE FORBIDS US FROM CHANGING THE PAST.

IT'S DIFFERENT HERE! THE SHINGOUZ MODIFIED THE PAST — WE'D ONLY BE ERASING THAT MODIFICATION. IT'S OUR ONLY WAY OUT, MR ALBERT.

PROBLEM IS, MR ALBERT SHOT UP OUR TELETRANSPORTER. THE NAVCOMPUTER IS ON THE FRITZ.

WAIT... **THAT'S** YOUR SPATIO-TEMPORAL NAVCOMPUTER?

YEAH, WELL, SOME OF US DON'T HAVE A BRAND-NEW SHIP PAID FOR BY GALAXITY.

WE DOLD YOU ... SNIFF ... DAD ID WAS BADCHED DOGEDER...

IT WORKED JUST FINE BEFORE MR ALBERT BLASTED IT!

WITH ANY LUCK I MIGHT BE ABLE TO REPAIR IT, BUT IT'LL TAKE TIME...

MR ALBERT AND I WILL TRY TO MEET WITH THAT SHA-OO — STALL FOR TIME.

YOU NEVER KNOW. MAYBE HE'LL AGREE TO NEGOTIATE.

17

GOOD LUCK — I HAVE A GOOD FEELING ABOUT THIS!

PFFF... IT'S ALL BLOWN TO BITS IN THERE! AND THE ANTIGRAV GENERATOR'S TOO SMALL...

IT'S CONSTANTLY OVERHEATING.

HOW WERE YOU EVEN ABLE TO...?

WOOOO! THE NEW MODEL OF POD-20 PSYCHIC OVERPRICER IS OUT!

ORDER ONE — IT'S ALWAYS HANDY.

DE OLD BODEL WAS ... SNIRFL ... DOO BIG...

HEY, DON'T BOTHER HELPING ME, OK?

WE'D LOVE TO ... BUT NOW THAT WE'VE DISCOVERED WE'RE ALLERGIC TO WORK...

HELLO, KIDS!

?

OH, ER... HELLO, BOSS.

SO, HOW'S THE MISSION GOING? HAVE YOU FOUND THE SCARY MR ZI-PONE?

UH... YES. WELL, IN PART, SO TO SPEAK, ALTHOUGH THE ESSENTIAL IS ... UH ... STILL OUT THERE. WE HAD A SLIGHT BLASTER MALFUNCTION AND...

HUH?!

THE HEAD WAS SWALLOWED BY A FISH.

WHAT?! WHAT ARE THOSE GUYS DOING THERE?

18 -

LISTEN, ER... WE'RE WORKING ON SOMETHING ELSE RIGHT NOW... A CARD GAME THAT WENT SIDEWAYS, AND...

WH... WHAT ARE YOU TALKING ABOUT, VALERIAN?! ZI-PONE'S HEAD HOLDS THE BANKING RECORDS OF BILLIONS OF SMALL SAVERS.

IT'S ALL INSIDE ST PERCENT AND GROSCERNIN, THE TWO NANO-SERVERS HIDDEN INSIDE HIS NOGGIN! IT'S ONE OF THE BUSIEST TAX HAVENS IN THE UNIVERSE! TOP PRIORITY, VALERIAN!

IF YOU DON'T FIND THAT HEAD, WE'RE FACING AN INTERGALACTIC ECONOMIC CRISIS!

WARS! SOLAR SYSTEMS LAID WASTE! WE CAN'T LEAVE ALL OF THAT INSIDE THE BELLY OF A FISH!

THE MISSION, VALERIAN! THE MISSION!

OK, FINE... I GUESS I'M FISHING QUANTUNA, THEN...

I'M COUNTING ON YOU! I'LL BE OFF ON COMPENSATORY TIME FOR A FEW DAYS, BUT DON'T HESITATE TO KEEP ME APPRISED. YOU CAN REACH ME ANY TIME – THAT'S THE PROBLEM WITH IMPLANTED COM UNITS.

I DON'T SUPPOSE YOU'VE GOT SOME SORT OF SONAR IN THIS LEMON?

19-

YOUR COCKTAIL, SIR.

PROBLEMS, HONEY?

NO, NO... IT'S NOTHING... WHAT ARE YOU DOING, EXACTLY?

I'M TRYING TO ADJUST THAT STUPID ANTIGRAV LIFEBELT. IT WAS EASIER WHEN YOU JUST HAD TO INFLATE THEM...

I DON'T WORK MY REAR END OFF 15 HOURS A DAY COMMANDING THE SPATIO-TEMPORAL SECRET SERVICE SO THAT MY SON WILL LOOK LIKE A YOKEL WITH AN INFLATABLE RING!

I WANT WHAT'S BEST FOR HIM! IT'S THE LATEST MODEL. COST ME A FORTUNE.

YEAH, BUT RIGHT NOW HE CAN'T EVEN GET INTO THE WATER...

GIMME THAT! PFF... CAN'T BE THAT HARD TO SORT OUT!

GRAH!... WHO CAME UP WITH THIS INTERFACE ?!...

YOU SEEM TENSE... TROUBLE AT WORK?

IT'S... THERE'S... I HAVE SOME PROBLEMS WITH THE SERVICE'S ACCOUNTING. SINCE WE HAD TO CUT DOWN ON PERSONNEL, I'VE BEEN MANAGING THE ACCOUNTS AND I MADE A FEW ... ER ... RISKY INVESTMENTS ... AND ... IT'S COMPLICATED.

INVESTMENTS? WITH WHAT MONEY? NOT THE AGENTS' PENSION FUND, I HOPE?

N... NO NEED TO WORRY YOURSELF OVER THAT, HONEY. ENJOY YOUR HOLIDAYS.

HE'LL COME DOWN EVENTUALLY – THE BATTERY'S ALMOST DEAD.

20-

I'M TELLING YOU — THE ANTIGRAV WON'T TAKE IT...

ARE YOU SURE THIS THING'S WORKING?

NO.

WE GOT IT FROM A TERRAN ORNITHO-LOGIST. HE USED IT TO FOLLOW THE MIGRATIONS OF RUFOUS-SIDED BROADBILLS, WHICH...

GKK... KRRRR... ...STER VALER... KRR...

I KNEW IT! MR ZI-PONE IS STILL ALIVE!

HELLO! HELLO?

ER... IF YOU EXPECT IT TO SERVE AS A PHONE TOO, I'M SORRY, BUT...

KRR... ...ELLY OF A FISHKRRRR... GGKRAAA... CORROSIVE ACKRRRCIRCUITS... SOS... KRRR...

HE'S MELTING! HARD TO LEFT!!

SHOULDN'T IT BE 'PORT' ON A SHIP?

OK, FINE — PORT!

IT WON'T GO THERE.

WHAT?

THE RUDDER'S STUCK.

THEN TURN STARBOARD THREE TIMES AND THAT'LL MAKE IT PORT!

HUH? WHAT'S HE TALKING ABOUT?...

21-

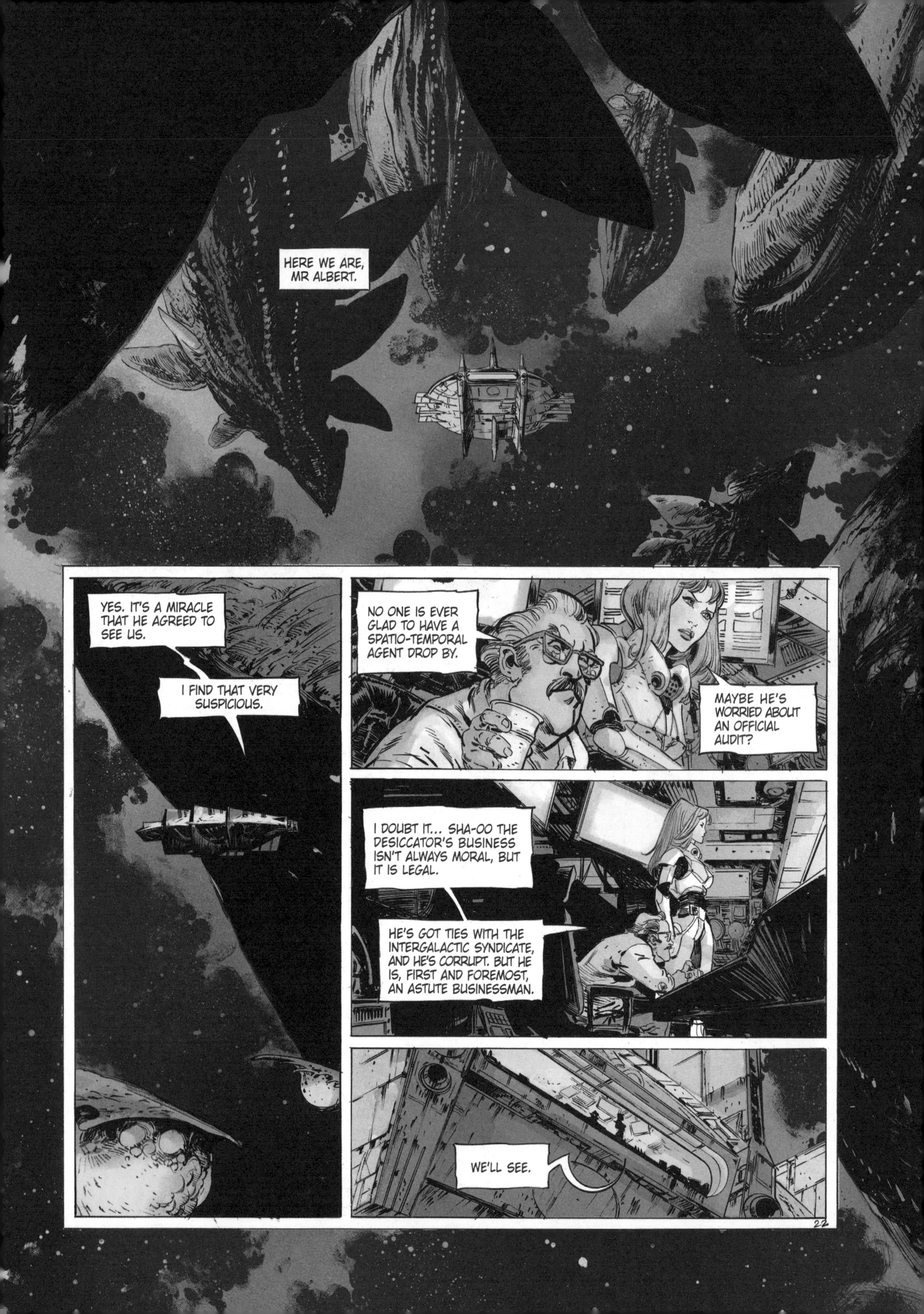
HERE WE ARE, MR ALBERT.
YES. IT'S A MIRACLE THAT HE AGREED TO SEE US.
I FIND THAT VERY SUSPICIOUS.
NO ONE IS EVER GLAD TO HAVE A SPATIO-TEMPORAL AGENT DROP BY.
MAYBE HE'S WORRIED ABOUT AN OFFICIAL AUDIT?
I DOUBT IT... SHA-OO THE DESICCATOR'S BUSINESS ISN'T ALWAYS MORAL, BUT IT IS LEGAL.
HE'S GOT TIES WITH THE INTERGALACTIC SYNDICATE, AND HE'S CORRUPT. BUT HE IS, FIRST AND FOREMOST, AN ASTUTE BUSINESSMAN.
WE'LL SEE.
22

I'LL LET VALERIAN KNOW WE'RE ALMOST THERE.

HELLO, VALERIAN? ARE THE REPAIRS NEARLY DONE?

WELL, NO, BECAUSE THE FOLKS IN GALAXITY ARE ASKING ME TO CATCH THAT BLUE TUNA, AND...

BUT, VALERIAN, EARTH IS MORE IMPORTANT THAN MR ZI-PONE'S ANONYMOUS BANK ACCOUNTS!

YOU MUST REPAIR THE SHINGOUZLOOZ'S TELETRANSPORTER!!

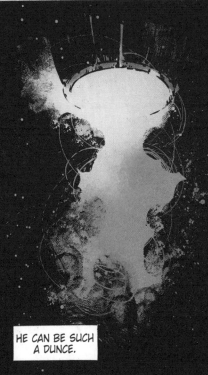

FINE, FINE! ALL RIGHT! PFFF... MAKE UP YOUR DAMN MINDS, ALL OF YOU!

HE CAN BE SUCH A DUNCE.

WELL, WE'RE ON, MR ALBERT.

I'M GETTING SICK AND TIRED OF THIS. DO THIS — NO, DO THAT...

THE NAVCOMPUTER'S STRUGGLING. IT'LL NEVER HOLD...

YES? WHAT NOW?

YOU'RE GETTING A CALL ON YOUR COMMUNICATOR, AND IT'S TRYING TO TRANSFER IT TO OUR SHIP'S HOLOCOM.

?

HULLO. I'M CALLING TO ASK WHAT TIME YOU'LL BE HERE WITH THE GOODS?

'CAUSE I HAVE A PRETTY TIGHT SCHEDULE, SO...

WHAT ... ARE YOU TALKING ABOUT, SIR?

THE QUANTUNA, OF COURSE. MY BOSS PAID IN ADVANCE — A HEFTY SUM, TOO.

HE WAS PROMISED THE ULTRA-FAST SPATIO-TEMPORAL TELEDELIVERY SERVICE.

THE THING IS, QUANTUNA MUST BE SERVED REALLY FRESH, SO...

HUH? WHAT THE... ER... WHO GAVE YOU MY NUMBER?

24-

THE MIDDLEMAN, OF COURSE... A COMPANY BASED IN ST PERCENT AND GROSCERNIN.

OH, YEAH, BUT... UM... THAT MIDDLE-MAN LOST HIS HEAD! AND I'M STILL TRYING TO LOCATE IT, ACTUALLY, AND ... ANYWAY, THERE WON'T BE A DELIVERY.

ARE YOU JOKING!? IN A FEW HOURS, THE LARGEST INTERGALACTIC CRIME SYNDICATE WILL BE COMING HERE FOR DINNER.

AND THAT QUANTUNA IS THE PIECE DE RESISTANCE OF MY MENU!

SOME OF THEM ARE COMING JUST TO SEE IF MY BOSS CAN REALLY AFFORD A QUANTUNA!!

!....

SUCH PEOPLE DO NOT TAKE KINDLY TO THIS SORT OF JOKE! YOU'D BETTER DELIVER IF YOU DON'T WANT A WHOLE ARMY OF KILLERS COMING AFTER YOU!

BAD NEWS, IS IT?

25

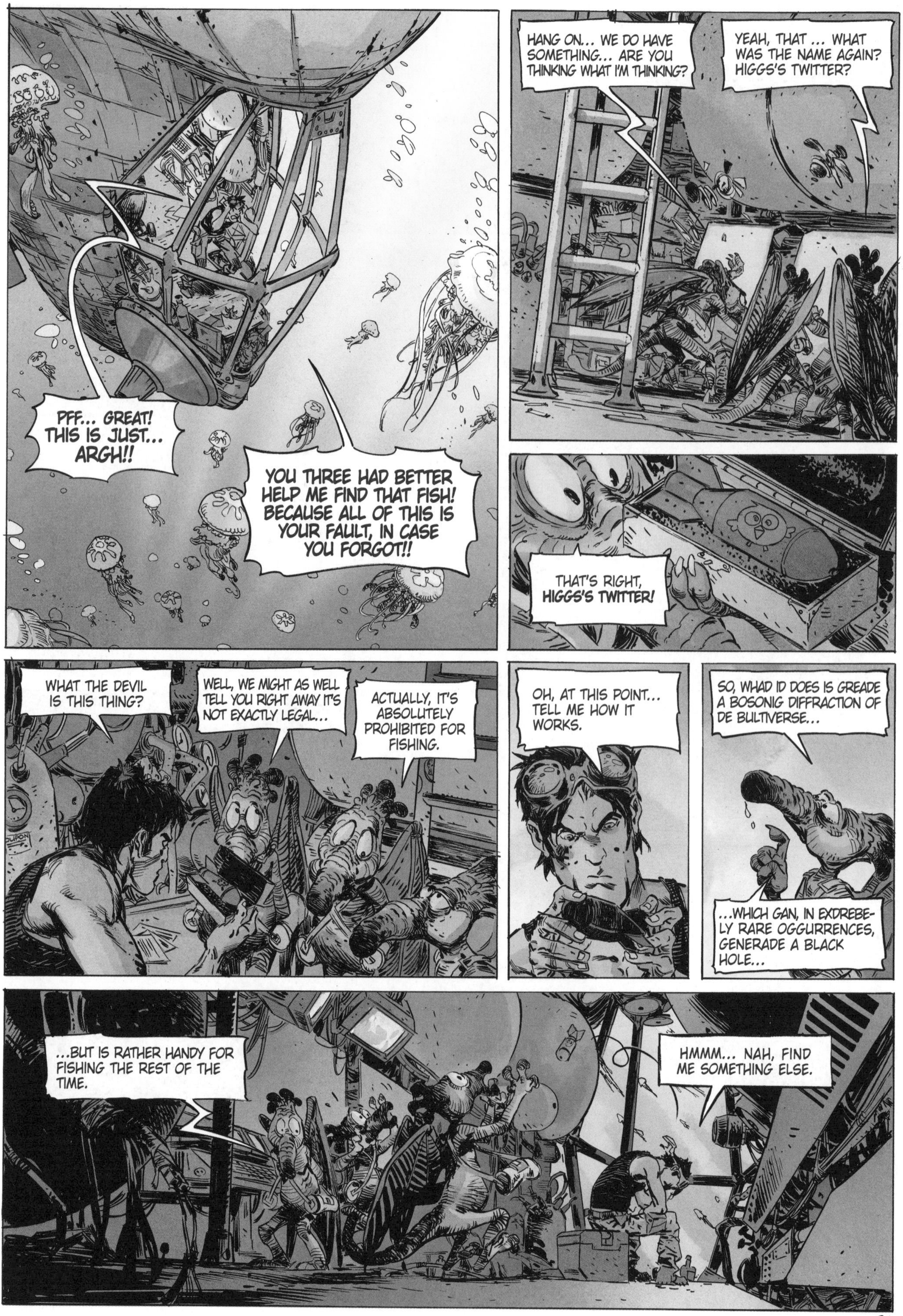

PFF... GREAT! THIS IS JUST... ARGH!!
YOU THREE HAD BETTER HELP ME FIND THAT FISH! BECAUSE ALL OF THIS IS YOUR FAULT, IN CASE YOU FORGOT!!
HANG ON... WE DO HAVE SOMETHING... ARE YOU THINKING WHAT I'M THINKING?
YEAH, THAT ... WHAT WAS THE NAME AGAIN? HIGGS'S TWITTER?
THAT'S RIGHT, HIGGS'S TWITTER!
WHAT THE DEVIL IS THIS THING?
WELL, WE MIGHT AS WELL TELL YOU RIGHT AWAY IT'S NOT EXACTLY LEGAL...
ACTUALLY, IT'S ABSOLUTELY PROHIBITED FOR FISHING.
OH, AT THIS POINT... TELL ME HOW IT WORKS.
SO, WHAD ID DOES IS GREADE A BOSONIG DIFFRACTION OF DE BULTIVERSE...
...WHICH GAN, IN EXDREBE-LY RARE OGGURRENCES, GENERADE A BLACK HOLE...
...BUT IS RATHER HANDY FOR FISHING THE REST OF THE TIME.
HMMM... NAH, FIND ME SOMETHING ELSE.

26 -

PFF... HOW DID ZI-PONE MANAGE TO BAG HIMSELF A QUANTUNA?

THAT'S ARTIFICIAL INTELLIGENCE FOR YOU.

IN THIS MAGAZINE, THEY SAY YOU NEED TO BAIT USING A CONTINUUWORM. IT'S AN ASTRAL MAGGOT THAT UNRAVELS THE FABRIC OF SPACE-TIME IN ORDER TO TRAVEL THROUGH IT.

IT TAKES THE HOOK INTO OTHER POTENTIAL REALITIES, WHERE THE QUANTUNAS CAN BE FOUND SWIMMING BETWEEN DIMENSIONS.

WHAT?! YOU MEAN FOR ALL WE KNOW, MY QUANTUNA ISN'T EVEN IN OUR REALITY?

THAT'S PRETTY MUCH HOW QUANTUM MIGRATION WORKS.

SO, WITHOUT A CONTINUUWORM, IT'S HOPELESS?

WELL ...

AND WHERE CAN WE FIND A CONTINUUWORM?

THEY SAY HERE THAT THE BEST PLACE TO GET ONE IS ... INSIDE A QUANTUNA'S STOMACH...

MEANWHILE, EARTH KEEPS CHANGING HANDS OVER OUR HEADS, AND A BUNCH OF KILLERS WILL SOON BE COMING HERE TO MURDER ME.

YEB! AD THE ANDIGRAV ENGINE... SNIRFL... IS GOING DO BLOW.

COME ON, VALERIAN, CHEER UP! IT COULD BE WORSE.

27-

WORSE? I DON'T SEE HOW...

THIS IS THE SORT OF WELCOME I LIKE.

IF HE AGREES TO SELL THE COMPANY BACK TO US, WHAT DO WE DO? HOW ARE WE GOING TO PAY HIM?

I HAVE A LITTLE SOMETHING PUT AWAY FOR A RAINY DAY, BUT I DON'T THINK IT'LL BE ENOUGH.

WE'LL IMPROVISE. THE MAIN THING IS TO BUY TIME.

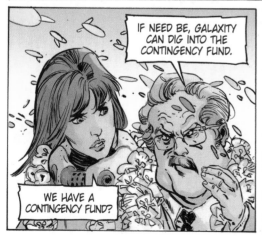

IF NEED BE, GALAXITY CAN DIG INTO THE CONTINGENCY FUND.

WE HAVE A CONTINGENCY FUND?

I BELIEVE SO.

28-

HA! HERE YOU ARE. DEAR LAURELINE! YOUR REPUTATION PALES BEFORE REALITY, IF I MAY SAY SO...

MY REPUTA- TION?

COME, NOW... DON'T ACT LIKE YOU DON'T KNOW. YOU ARE THE STAR OF SPATIO- TEMPORAL AGENTS.

YOUR BEAUTY IS CELEBRATED ACROSS THE UNIVERSE.

IT... IT IS?

YOU CANNOT IMAGINE HOW DELIGHTED I AM TO MEET YOU.

AND THIS IS THE FAMOUS VALERIAN, I SUPPOSE?

HUH? OH, NO, THIS IS MR ALBERT.

THAT MAKES MORE SENSE...

I DIDN'T QUITE UNDERSTAND YOUR REASON FOR COMING... WHAT EXACTLY CAN I DO FOR YOU, DELICIOUS LAURELINE?

WELL, HERE'S THE SITUATION... YOU'VE RECENTLY ACQUIRED A COMPANY...

SHINGOUZLOOZ INC.

29 -

OH, THAT? PAH... CAN'T WIN THEM ALL, I GUESS. THAT'LL TEACH ME TO LET THE GAMBLING BUG BITE ME.

I DON'T UNDERSTAND. AREN'T YOU HAPPY WITH YOUR ACQUISITION?

EARTH SHOULD BE A GODSEND FOR A WATER BROKER. IT'S COVERED IN A BILLION BILLION CUBIC METRES OF WATER, AND...

AND NOTHING! OH, I TOO STARTED DREAMING WHEN I REALISED WHAT I'D OBTAINED!

JUST BY SELLING ONE THIRD OF ALL THE WATER ON EARTH, I'D HAVE BECOME ONE OF THE RICHEST MEN IN THE UNIVERSE. BUT I'VE HAD TO ACCEPT THE TRUTH: THAT WATER IS UNSELLABLE.

IT IS? BUT WHY?

BECAUSE OF YOU TERRANS!

YOU'VE ONLY BEEN ON EARTH FOR A FEW MILLENNIA, BUT A COUPLE OF HUNDRED YEARS WAS ENOUGH FOR YOU TO UTTERLY POLLUTE YOUR MAIN RESOURCE!

BEEP... BEEP... BEEEP... BEEP... BEEP!

THE STAR PORPOISES WE ALWAYS SEND AHEAD TO SCOUT CAME BACK SICK...!

BIIIIIIIIP!!!B

30 —

32

...THEIR BODIES FULL OF PLASTIC PARTICLES, HORMONE DISRUPTORS, HEAVY METALS!

THOSE THAT CAME BACK.

FIVE HAVE DIED ALREADY...

CREATURES THAT HAD LIVED THOUSANDS OF YEARS.

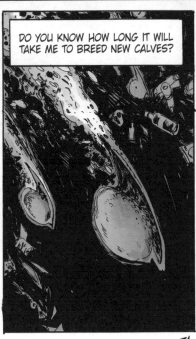

DO YOU KNOW HOW LONG IT WILL TAKE ME TO BREED NEW CALVES?

FIVE HUNDRED EARTH YEARS!

31

CAPTAIN SHA-OO... THAT PORPOISE DIDN'T MAKE IT EITHER...

SO THAT'S SIX LOST ASSETS.

I DON'T UNDERSTAND HOW HUMANS MANAGED TO DEGRADE THE ONE SUBSTANCE INDISPENSABLE TO THEIR OWN EXISTENCE IN SUCH A SHORT TIME.

YES, OUR CIVILISATION HAS BEEN ... SOMEWHAT...

OH, HOW I WISH I COULD SEND THOSE CREATURES BACK TO EARTH'S PAST, TO SIPHON THAT WATER WHEN IT WAS STILL PURE!

FOR, ELSEWHERE IN THE UNIVERSE, THERE ARE PEOPLE WHO WOULD PAY A HIGH PRICE FOR WATER OF THAT QUALITY. AND THEY'D TAKE GOOD CARE OF IT, BELIEVE ME.

ALAS, IT'S IMPOSSIBLE. MY CREATURES CANNOT SURVIVE SPATIO-TEMPORAL TRAVEL.

WELL, LISTEN, WE'RE SORRY TO HEAR SUCH SAD NEWS, AND ... TO COMPENSATE YOU, IF YOU WANT, WE'D BE WILLING TO BUY THE COMPANY FROM YOU.

FOR... UH...

AH, DEAR LAURELINE.

THANK YOU FOR YOUR GENEROSITY, BUT, YOU SEE, I DO NOT NEED YOUR MONEY. YOUR MERE PRESENCE HERE IS ENOUGH.

HUH? WHAT DO YOU MEAN?

THE COMMUNITY OF YOUR ADMIRERS, LAURELINE. **THAT** IS THE TRUE OPPORTUNITY STEMMING FROM THIS RISKY TRANSACTION.

THERE ARE THOUSANDS OF FORUMS DEDICATED TO YOU ON THE INTERWEBS...

TO THE POINT THAT SEVERAL COMPANIES ARE ATTEMPTING TO CREATE SYNTHETIC VERSIONS OF YOU TO SATISFY THE DEMAND.

WHAT? THE 'DEMAND'?! OH, THE CREEPS! THEY HAVE NO RIGHT!!

NO, THEY DON'T, AND THAT'S THE PROBLEM. THE LAWS ON GENOMIC PROPERTY ARE EXTREMELY STRICT: EVEN IF SOMEONE MANAGED TO CLONE YOU, COMMERCIALISATION WITHOUT YOUR CONSENT WOULD BE FORBIDDEN.

I DAMN WELL HOPE SO!

YOU SEEM TO KNOW A LOT ABOUT COMMERCIAL LEGISLATION.

IT'S MY JOB — KNOWING THE LAWS SO I CAN FIND OPPORTUNITIES; BUYING, SELLING ACROSS THE UNIVERSE...

AND, AS IT HAPPENS, NOW THAT I AM THE OWNER OF EARTH, I ALSO OWN ALL LIFE THAT COMES FROM IT.

INCLUDING YOUR GENETIC CODE, LAURELINE.

SEE? THE SENSORS EMBEDDED IN YOUR FLOWER GARLAND HAVE FINISHED THEIR MAPPING.

I'M NOW GOING TO CLONE YOU MASSIVELY...

...AND PUT YOU UP FOR SALE ALL OVER THE GALAXY...

...IN A WIDE RANGE OF OPTIONS.

33-

GH...

URFF!...

SORRY TO RUIN YOUR LITTLE PROJECT, MASTER SHA-OO THE DESICCATOR...

...BUT I INTEND TO REMAIN THE ONE AND ONLY!

GG...

G...

GUARDS...

RUN, MR ALBERT!

...SOUND ... THE ...
ALAAAARM!!!

LITTLE PEST!

SHE DESTROYED EVERYTHING!

KILL HER!

ALL I NEED IS HER GENOME!!!

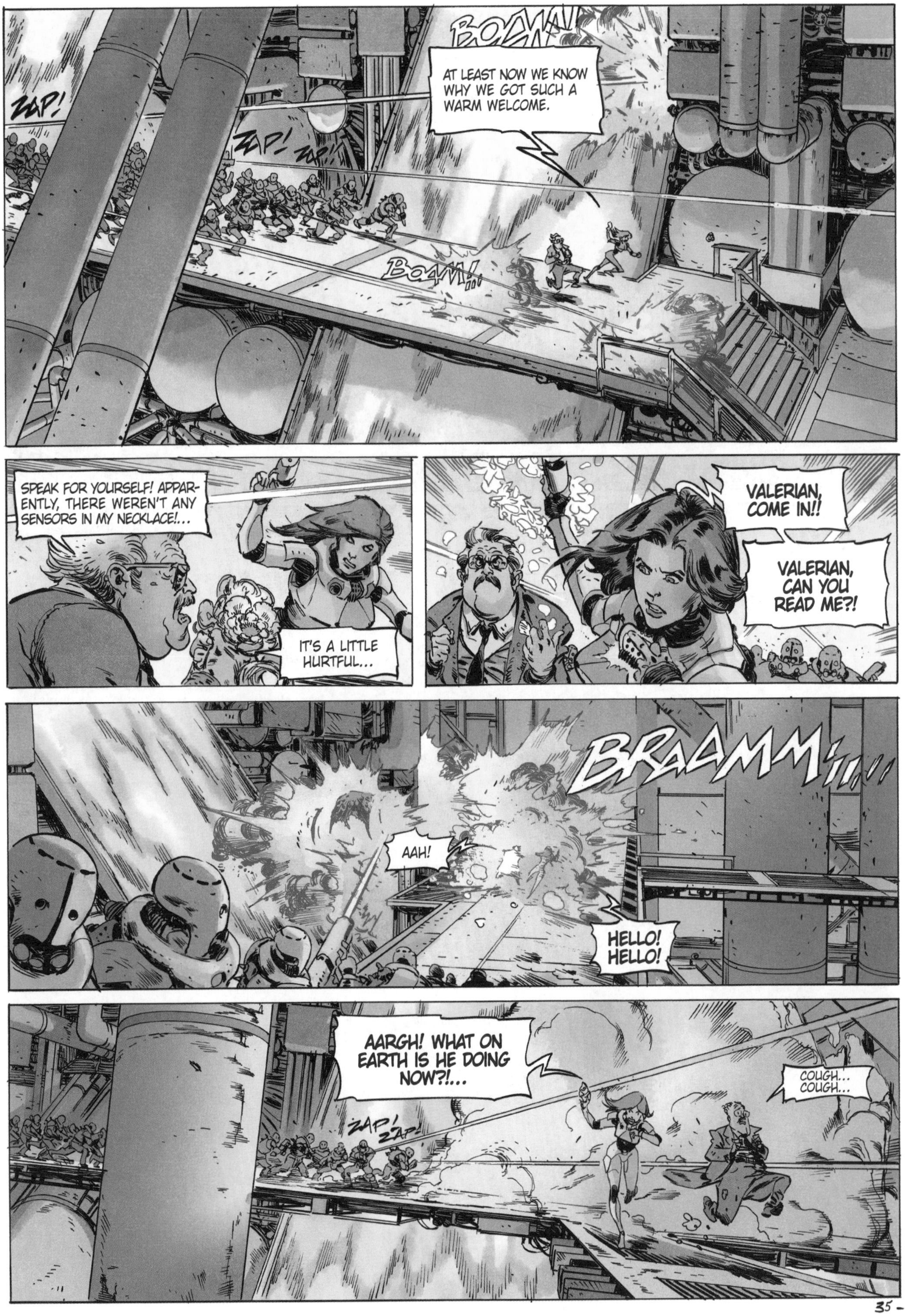
BOOM!
ZAP!
AT LEAST NOW WE KNOW WHY WE GOT SUCH A WARM WELCOME.
ZAP!
ZAP!
BOOM!
SPEAK FOR YOURSELF! APPARENTLY, THERE WEREN'T ANY SENSORS IN MY NECKLACE!...
IT'S A LITTLE HURTFUL...
VALERIAN, COME IN!!
VALERIAN, CAN YOU READ ME?!
BRAAMM!!!
AAH!
HELLO! HELLO!
AARGH! WHAT ON EARTH IS HE DOING NOW?!...
COUGH... COUGH...
ZAP! ZAP!
35

HELLO, LAURELINE?! IS THAT YOU? I CAN'T HEAR YOU – I ... I'M GOING THROUGH A TUNNEL... PFF...

AAAND IT CUT OFF. SHINGOUZ, MY BOYS, WE NEED TO FIND A WAY OUT OF HERE.

YEAH, BUT ... APART FROM USING HIGGS'S TWITTER...

KRRF...TER VALERIAN... KRRRRR...KRR... HERE...KRR...

?!

MR ZI-PONE! IS THAT YOU?!...

ZZZOF COURSE GZT, WHO ELSE ... COULD ... KRRR... IT BE?...

WE'VE GOT IT!

WE'VE GOT IT!

HERE HE IS! HOLD THE FISH, GUYS!

36.

BLURGH! THIS REMINDS ME OF HELPING A FEMALE GLÜPMORV... GULP...

...GAHH... THROUGH A DIFFICULT BIRTHING DURING THE SIEGE OF THE ASTEROID OF... OH... OH... I...!

...I'VE GOT IT!

HAHAHA!! WOOHOO!

GZZT...

...RRAAABOUT TIME...

YOU'VE GOT TO ADMIT — IT'S A REAL STROKE OF LUCK FINDING YOU INSIDE THIS FISH...

NOT XLXLUCK. DJZ! TOOK CONTROL OF THE XQUANTUNA'S NERVOUS SYXSXSTEM SO IT'D THROW ITSELF DOWN THE GULLET OF THIS CREATURE.

OH? AND HOW DID YOU DO THAT?

SHORT-ZZFREQUENCY BRAINWAVES... ZZTT... THEN I TOOK OVER THE BIGGERRRRZ CREATURE'S NERVOUS SYSTEM SO IT'D GO AND SSS... WALLOW YOUR SHIP...

H... HUH... SO, YOU CAN CONTROL PEOPLE, JUST LIKE THAT?

NOT PEOPLE. TOO MANY GRZZT NEURONAL CONNECTIONS. BUT PRIMITIVE CREATURES, EASY. REDUCED CONNECTOME.

SO, THOSE WEASELS THERE, COULD YOU CONTROL THEM?

JZZZZT... THINK SO, BUT NOT IN MY ZKRCURRENT STATE.

YEAH, RIGHT! IN YOUR DREAMS, YOU PHONY! HOW ABOUT I SMACK YOU IN THE FACE WITH A TIN OPENER?

NO ONE'S EVER CONTROLLED A SHINGOUZ'S MIND! NOT EVEN A SHINGOUZ!

NO NEED FOR VIOLENCE, FRIENDS! WITH THIS TIN HEAD, I'LL BE ABLE TO REPAIR YOUR NAVCOMPUTER!

GET READY — WE WON'T BE STICKING AROUND.

HOLD ON! WE'RE NOT GOING TO LEAVE THIS HERE — IT COSTS TOO MUCH...

37-

ZAP!
ZAP!
ZAP!

THIS TIME IT'S OVER, MY DEAR.

I'M GOING TO TRIGGER THE POLONIUM 210 BOMB HIDDEN IN MY FOUR-COLOUR PEN...

WE'LL BE INSTANTLY VAPOR-ISED AND LEAVE NOTHING FOR THOSE DNA LOOTERS.

HELLO?...

LAURELINE? CAN YOU HEAR ME?

VALERIAN!!

IT'S ABOUT TIME! WHAT HAVE YOU BEEN DOING?!

WHICH COLOUR IS THE DETONATOR AGAIN...?

IT'S OK! I'VE REPAIRED THE SHINGOUZ'S NAVCOMPUTER! I'M HEADING STRAIGHT TO THE TRANSFER LOCATION TO INTERCEPT THE PROBE.

ZFFFTTTXXX...

IN A FEW MINUTES, EARTH WILL BE FREE AGAIN.

NOT IF THIS THING BLOWS UP FIRST...

WELL DONE, SWEETIE! I KNEW YOU COULD DO IT!

38_

WHAT...!? LAURELINE, WHAT ARE YOU DOING?

COME ON, MR ALBERT. NO NEED TO RISK OUR LIVES POINTLESSLY.

THE GAME IS OVER.

LET'S GO AND HAVE SOME FUN WITH THAT TWO-BIT CLONED MEAT MERCHANT.

GET READY. SLIDING INTO THE MULTIVERSE IN FIVE...

FOUR...

THREE...

TWO...

ONE...

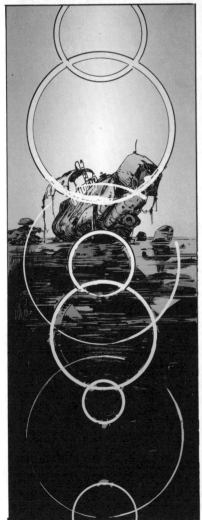

GROOI GARGL

BJURP...

39

41

HERE WE ARE.

SO, THIS IS EARTH AS IT WAS BEFORE LIFE APPEARED...

I DIDN'T THINK IT WAS POSSIBLE TO GO THIS FAR BACK IN TIME.

O THINK THAT
BEFORE OUR
E FATE OF...

WOOHOOO!!! I'LL TAKE ONE TOO!

HREE!

ARE YOU EVEN LISTENING?

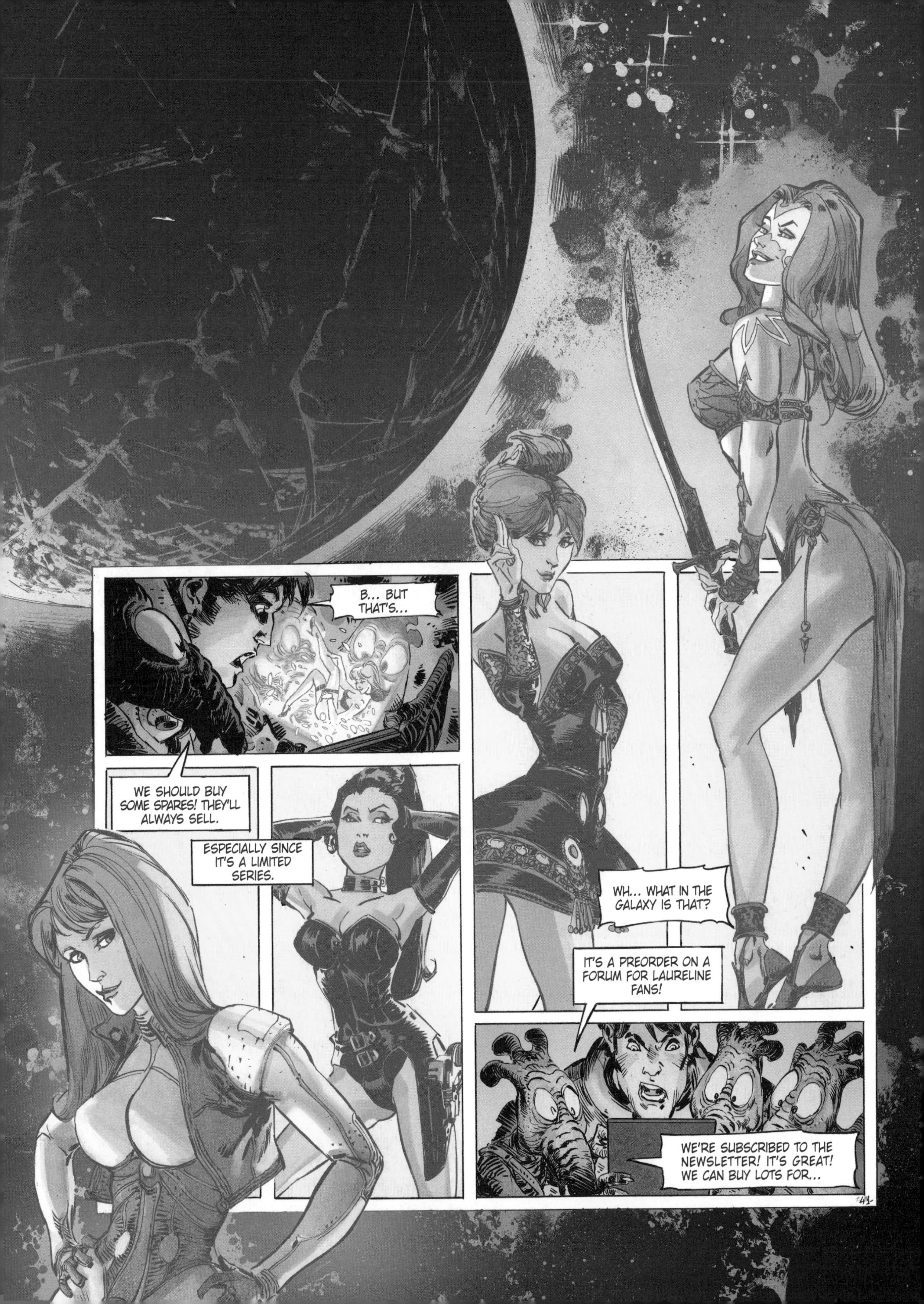

B... BUT THAT'S...
WE SHOULD BUY SOME SPARES! THEY'LL ALWAYS SELL.
ESPECIALLY SINCE IT'S A LIMITED SERIES.
WH... WHAT IN THE GALAXY IS THAT?
IT'S A PREORDER ON A FORUM FOR LAURELINE FANS!
WE'RE SUBSCRIBED TO THE NEWSLETTER! IT'S GREAT! WE CAN BUY LOTS FOR...
41

DON'T YOU CREEPS THINK WE'VE GOT BETTER THINGS TO DO THAN BUY A BUNCH OF LAURELINE TOYS?!

OH, BUT THOSE AREN'T TOYS. THEY'RE REAL LAURELINES! LOOK, IT'S RIGHT THERE: 100 PERCENT ORGANIC.

HUH? BUT THAT'S IMPOSSIBLE!

THE PROBE IS ABOUT TO ARRIVE!

I WISH WE DIDN'T HAVE TO DESTROY IT. THE ONE TIME WE BUILD SOMETHING OURSELVES AND IT WORKS...

NOD DO BEDTION WE RUID OUR HEALTH BUDDING ID DOGEDER.

YEAH, WELL, WATCH YOUR PRECIOUS PROBE AS I SLAM THIS JUNKER RIGHT INTO IT!

THERE IT IS!

LAURELINE, I'M ON SITE – AND SO'S THE PROBE. WE'RE RIGHT ON TRACK.

DEAR LAURELINE!

PERFECT...

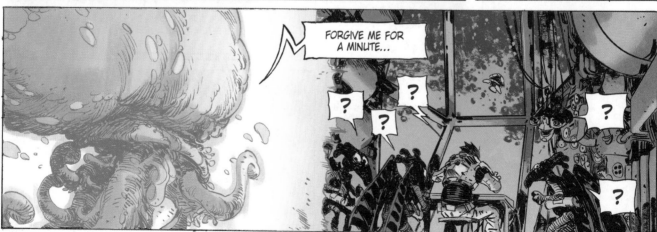

FORGIVE ME FOR A MINUTE...

? ? ? ? ?

42-

44

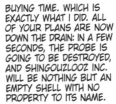

SUCH A PATHETIC ESCAPE ATTEMPT. WHAT WERE YOU HOPING TO ACCOMPLISH?

BUYING TIME. WHICH IS EXACTLY WHAT I DID. ALL OF YOUR PLANS ARE NOW DOWN THE DRAIN: IN A FEW SECONDS, THE PROBE IS GOING TO BE DESTROYED, AND SHINGOUZLOOZ INC. WILL BE NOTHING BUT AN EMPTY SHELL WITH NO PROPERTY TO ITS NAME.

MEANING YOU WILL OWN NOTHING.

NOT EARTH, NOT MY GENETIC CODE.

YOU'VE LOST, SHA-OO.

HMM... I SEE. YOUR REPUTATION IS WELL DESERVED, DEAR LAURELINE.

BUT I STILL HAVE ONE CARD TO PLAY.

WHAT ARE YOU DOING?

THAT COMPANY IS STILL WORTH A GOOD DEAL FOR A FEW MORE SECONDS, ISN'T IT?

TAP TAP TAP TAP TAP TAP! TAP! TAP!

THERE. I JUST UNLOADED SHINGOUZLOOZ INC. ON THE INTERGALACTIC MARKET.

WHAT? YOU SOLD THE COMPANY KNOWING IT HAD ALREADY LOST ALL VALUE?! THAT'S AGAINST THE COMMERCIAL LAWS OF—

IT'S ONLY AN OFFENCE IF YOU CAN PROVE IT, DEAR FELLOW.

THE BUYER MADE A GREAT DEAL. WELL, FOR A FEW MORE SECONDS, HAHAHA! AS FOR ME, I GOT A FEW MILLION CREDITS BACK.

NOT BAD FOR SELLING THE OBSOLETE DEED TO A DYING PLANET!

HHAHHAHAHHHHA!

GOOD FOR YOU. GOODBYE!

VALERIAN? HURRY UP AND DESTROY THAT PROBE SO WE CAN BE DONE WITH THIS WHOLE THING.

VALERIAN?

43-

WHAT? GALAXITY KNOWS ABOUT THE PROBE?

MMYES, I MUST CONFESS.

SO WHY DIDN'T THE BOSS TELL ME ABOUT IT?

HE DOESN'T KNOW. OUR FILE ON THE SITUATION IS COMPLETELY CONFIDENTIAL.

PREPOSTEROUS, ISN'T IT? EARTH NOW BELONGS TO THAT COMPANY — THE SHINGULAG OR SOME SUCH THING...

GOUZ-LOOZ.

SHINGOUZLOOZ.

BROBER BRODUDCIATION, BLEASE.

THAT MEANS YOU COULD HAVE PUT A STOP TO IT THIS WHOLE TIME? LIKE I'M TRYING TO DO?

YES, BUT WE DIDN'T.

I CAN SEE YOU DIDN'T, THANK YOU. WHAT I DON'T UNDERSTAND IS WHY NOT?

BECAUSE OF HIM.

BE?

YOU SEE, WHEN THE SHINGOUZ BUILT THEIR PROBE, THEY APPARENTLY DIDN'T CONCERN THEMSELVES MUCH WITH WHAT IT COULD CARRY ON ITS TRIP.

BUT THAT SHINGOUZ WITH THE VERY STUFFY NOSE THERE MUST HAVE SNEEZED A LOT THAT DAY.

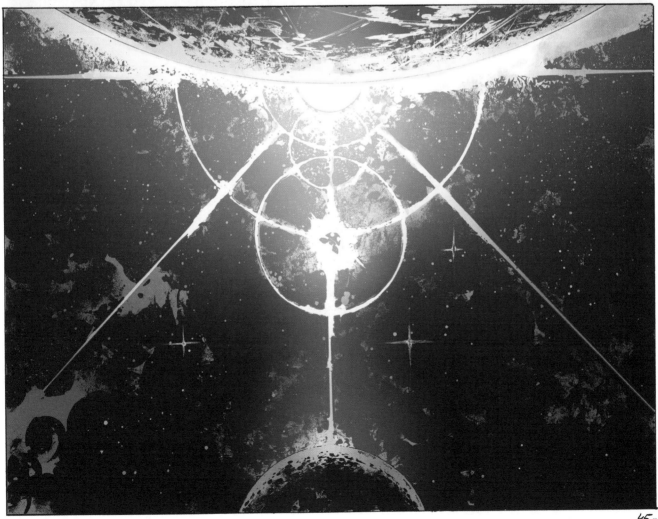

SORRY...

I DON'T UNDERSTAND...

YOU DON'T UNDERSTAND?

VALERIAN, ACCORDING TO OUR CALCULATIONS, THE ORIGINS OF LIFE ON EARTH, THREE AND A HALF BILLION YEARS AGO...

BROOF...

...HAPPEN TO BE PRECISELY THAT PROBE AND ITS UNUSUAL CARGO OF ALIEN MUCUS...

WHAT?

THE FIRST BACTERIA...

THE FIR...?! SHINGOUZ SNOT? LIFE ON EARTH COMES FROM SHINGOUZ SNOT??

WE'RE NOT ABSOLUTELY CERTAIN, BUT WE CANNOT TAKE ANY CHANCES.

IF YOU WERE TO DESTROY THAT PROBE, VALERIAN...

...THERE IS A POSSIBILITY THAT TERRAN LIFE AS WE KNOW IT...

...WOULD NEVER EVOLVE.

WELL, HOW ABOUT THAT!? WE'RE KIND OF YOUR GREAT-GRANDDADS, VALERIAN!

ISN'T THAT GREAT?

LED'S HUG DO CELEBRATE!

WELL, VALERIAN? IS THAT PROBE DESTROYED YET?

ER, NO.

NO?! WHAT DO YOU MEAN, NO?!

WE... WE CAN'T DESTROY IT... WE MUSTN'T... IT'S... IT'D TAKE TOO LONG TO EXPLAIN RIGHT NOW.

WHAT ARE WE GONNA DO, THEN? SHA-OO'S SOLD OFF THE COMPANY — AND WE DON'T EVEN KNOW TO WHOM!

OH, CRAP...

WELL, I'M DONE HERE. GOOD DAY.

I HOPE YOU'RE PROUD OF YOURSELVES! DO YOU HAVE ANY IDEA OF THE SPATIO-TEMPORAL MESS YOU'VE MADE!??...

...YOU AND YOUR BIG SNOT-FILLED NOSES!!?...

OH, HEY, COME ON! IT'S NOT A CRIME TO BE SNUFFLY, OK?!...

WE GREADED LIFE, YOU KNOW!

YOU'RE JEALOUS!!

UM... IFXXXX I MAY BE SO BRXFROLD...

I KN... KNNNOW WHO THE KRRRK NEW OWNER OF EARTH IS.

HUH? WHO IS IT?

XVZZYOU, VALERIAN.

XVZZME...?

SNIRFLL... XVZZHIB?

YES! I FOLLOWED GZIT YOUR CONVERSATIONS, AND WHEN I BWZBSAW SHA-OO'S OFFER APPEAR ON THE MARKET, I SEIZED THE OKXPPORTUNITY.

I'M STILL CONNECTED TO THE GLOBAL MARKET, YOU KNOW...

YOU DID TSZSSAVE MY LIFE, AFTER ALL... I BOUGHT EARTH WITH YOUR GZIIIT ACCOUNT.

MY ACCOUNT?

THE ONE I KCCXCREATED FOR YOU BEFORE I WAS ... PARTISZSTIONED.

IT'S THE ONLY ONE THAT WAS STILL IN MY SHORT-TERM GZIIIT MEMORY.

48-

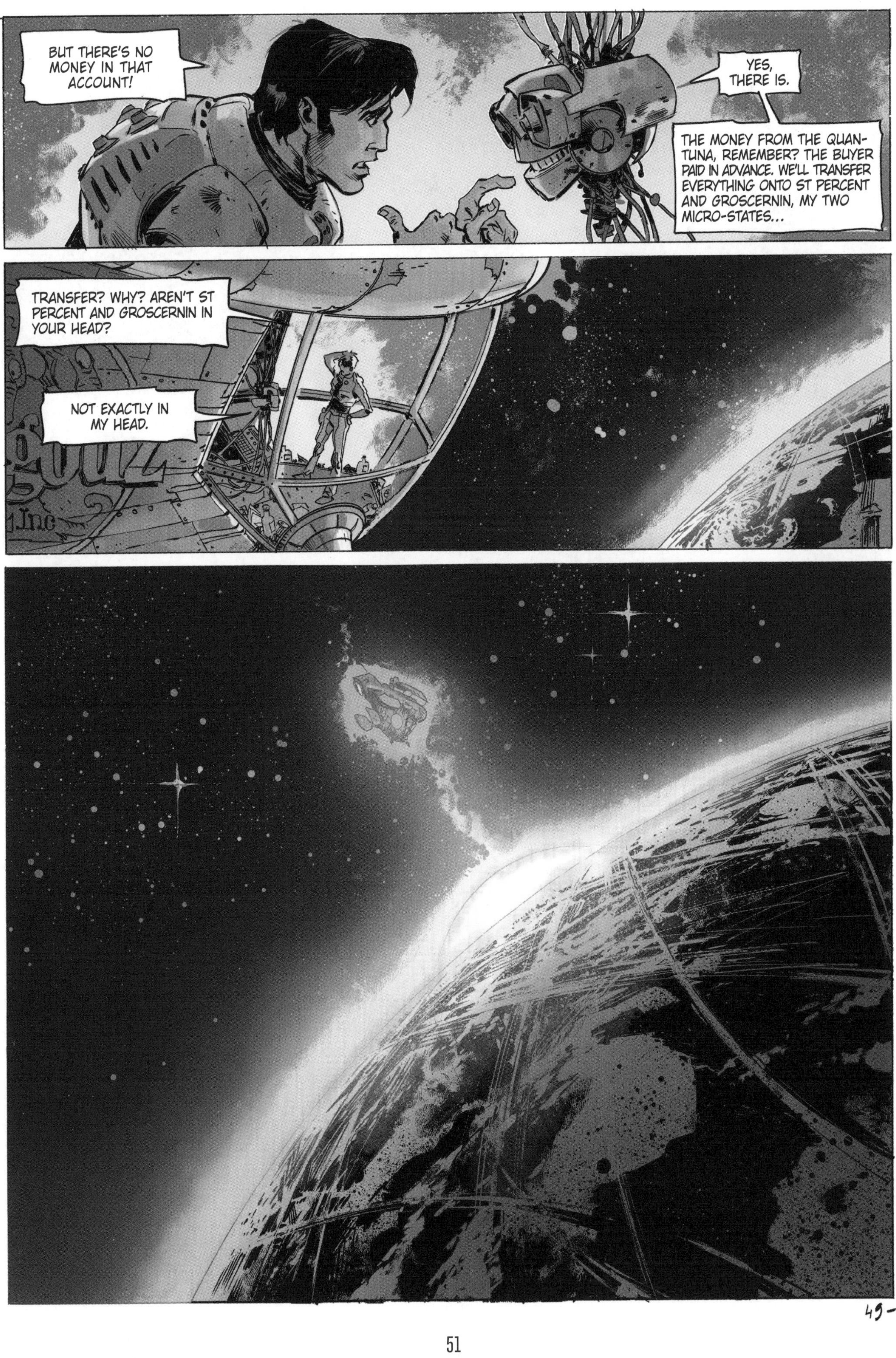
BUT THERE'S NO MONEY IN THAT ACCOUNT!
YES, THERE IS.
THE MONEY FROM THE QUANTUNA, REMEMBER? THE BUYER PAID IN ADVANCE. WE'LL TRANSFER EVERYTHING ONTO ST PERCENT AND GROSCERNIN, MY TWO MICRO-STATES...
TRANSFER? WHY? AREN'T ST PERCENT AND GROSCERNIN IN YOUR HEAD?
NOT EXACTLY IN MY HEAD.

FSHHHTT! GO ON, SHOO, YOU NASTY CRITTERS!

ALL RIGHT, ZI-PONE, TELL ME. WHAT MUST I DO?

ER...

ARE YOU SURE?

PULL MY SHORTS DOWN.

ST PERCENT AND GROSCERNIN.

YOU THINK YOU'RE FUNNY, I IMAGINE?

WHAT? ISN'T THAT WHAT YOU TERRANS CALL BEING 'BALLSY'?

WE'RE AGREED, THEN? I VALIDATE THE TRANSACTION, AND IN EXCHANGE YOU DROP ALL CHARGES AGAINST ME?

IT'S NOT LIKE WE HAVE A CHOICE.

50-

AND IT'S DONE. NOW I SUGGEST YOU DELIVER THE FISH WHILE IT'S STILL FRESH.

YOU HAVE LESS THAN AN HOUR LEFT.

OTHERWISE YOU'LL HAVE TO RETURN THE MONEY – AND ALL YOU HAVE LEFT IS EARTH, SO TO SPEAK.

WE'LL TAKE CARE OF THE DELIVERY FOR YOU! NOW THAT OUR FINE SHIP IS REPAIRED, WE'LL BE TRAVELLING EVERYWHERE!!

YAHOOO!

THEIR SHIP IS REPAIRED?

YEAH, I WAS ABLE TO GET IT TO WORK BY CONNECTING IT TO ZI-PONE'S HEAD, WHICH...

...WHICH ...

BAOOOMM...

51 –

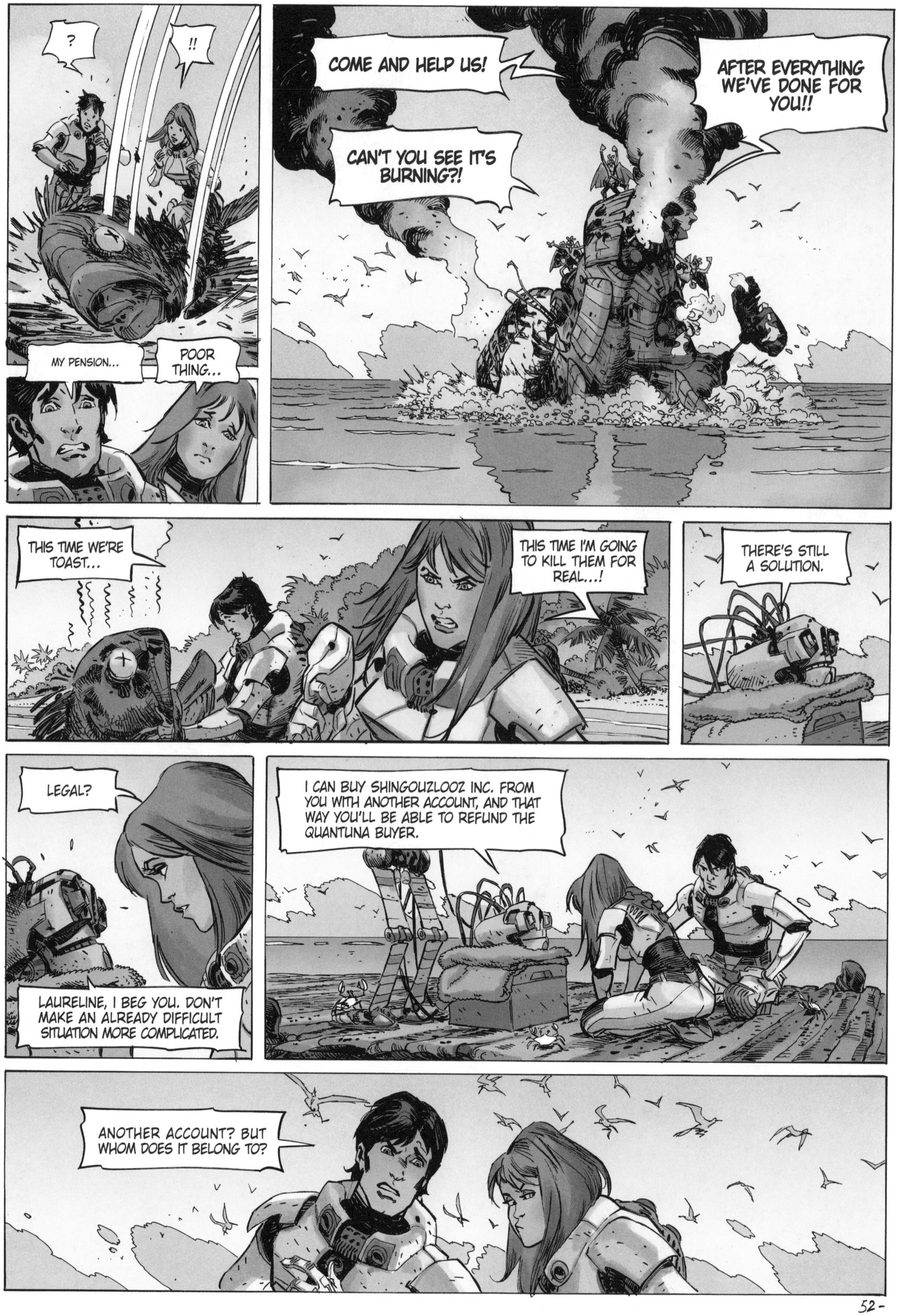
?
!!
MY PENSION...
POOR THING...
COME AND HELP US!
CAN'T YOU SEE IT'S BURNING?!
AFTER EVERYTHING WE'VE DONE FOR YOU!!
THIS TIME WE'RE TOAST...
THIS TIME I'M GOING TO KILL THEM FOR REAL...!
THERE'S STILL A SOLUTION.
LEGAL?
LAURELINE, I BEG YOU. DON'T MAKE AN ALREADY DIFFICULT SITUATION MORE COMPLICATED.
I CAN BUY SHINGOUZLOOZ INC. FROM YOU WITH ANOTHER ACCOUNT, AND THAT WAY YOU'LL BE ABLE TO REFUND THE QUANTUNA BUYER.
ANOTHER ACCOUNT? BUT WHOM DOES IT BELONG TO?
52-

GNNNNN
...

GNNNNNHH
...

OH, CUT IT OUT. YOU'RE NOT FUNNY.

SO, KIDS? HAVE YOU MANAGED TO RECOVER THAT EVIL FINANCIAL GENIUS?

OH, YES, AND I HAVE A QUESTION FOR YOU.

HOW SERIOUS WOULD IT BE, DO YOU THINK, IF EARTH BELONGED TO A SUBSIDIARY OF A CONTINGENCY FUND MANAGED BY GALAXITY AND DOMICILED IN A HIGH-FREQUENCY BRASS-PLATED CYBER-TESTICULAR TAX HAVEN ... HIDDEN INSIDE A PAIR OF SHORTS?...

HUH? WH...

...ASSUMING, OF COURSE, SOMEONE IN GALAXITY WOULD HAVE BEEN RECKLESS ENOUGH TO INVEST THAT FUND SO CARELESSLY...

WELL, UH... I SUPPOSE THAT ... IT'S, HUH, IT COULD BE A LOT WORSE, AND ... THE IMPORTANT THING IS THAT...

THAT?

GLP... THAT ALL OF THIS STAYS BETWEEN US.

ARE YOUR PROBLEMS FIXED, DARLING? FEELING BETTER ABOUT YOUR INVESTMENTS?

HMM... YES, IT'S... IN THE END, WE INVESTED IN SOMETHING WORTHWHILE.

53-

SERIOUSLY? YOU'RE GOING TO LEAVE US HERE?

ABSOLUTELY! I'VE LEFT YOU SOME TOOLS. I'M SURE YOU CAN COBBLE TOGETHER SOMETHING THAT FLIES FROM THE TWO WRECKS.

BUT THAT'LL TAKE US AGES.

GOOD! WHILE YOU'RE DOWN HERE, YOU'RE NOT ANYWHERE ELSE.

BUT WE'RE ALLERGIC TO MANUAL LABOUR!!

ACHOOO!

THERE! SEE WHAT YOU'VE DONE?!

HEY, WAIT A MINUTE... THIS PLANET IS TEEMING WITH BLUE TUNAS!

I'LL GO AND GET THE TWITTER...